- listening to audio versions of the story (e.g. Talking Stories)
- hearing the story read to them by others as they follow the printed text.

Rereading and rehearing helps children develop automatic word recognition and gives them models of fluent, expressive reading.

Comprehension strategies

Story	Comprehension strategies taught through these Group/Guided Reading Notes				
	Prediction	Questioning	Clarifying	Summarising	Imagining
In the Garden		✓	✓	✓	✓
Kipper and the Giant	✓	✓	✓	✓	✓
The Outing	✓	✓	✓	✓	
Land of the Dinosaurs	✓	✓	✓	✓	✓
Robin Hood	✓	✓	✓	✓	✓
The Treasure Chest	✓	✓	✓	✓	

Vocabulary and phonic opportunities

Each story contains many decodable words, providing lots of opportunities to practise phonic and word recognition skills. The chart shows the tricky words used in each book. The tricky words are common but do not conform to the phonic rules taught up to this point – children will need support to learn and recognise them. If children struggle with one of these words you can model how to read it.

In the Garden	Tricky words	bottle, called, can't, climb, desert, giant, jungle, love, mend, mountain, paw, pull(ed), push(ed), rain, strawberries
Kipper and the Giant	Tricky words	adventure, again, called, castle, giant, nobody, one, out, people, pointed, programme, signpost, their, threw, tiny, village
The Outing	Tricky words	apatosaurus, called, crocodiles, dinosaurs, elephants, home, hope, lady, museum, photograph, pictures, rain, room, school, shoe, some, zoo
Land of the Dinosaurs	Tricky words	another, apatosaurus, climbed, called, dinosaurs, eat, enormous, fierce, flew, found, good, meet, museum, one, our, photograph, push, school, some
Robin Hood	Tricky words	Anneena, called, can't, cheer, do, good, guitar, new, next, nobody, one, out, pantomime, people, recorder, Sheriff, some, suddenly, there, took, village, what, where, who, wood
The Treasure Chest	Tricky words	air, blew, called, close, colours, dangerous, good, jellyfish, lengths, little, lovely, many, more, necklace, new, next, octopus, our, out, passed, pull(ed), push(ed), some, surprise, there, thought, treasure, were, what, who

Group/Guided Reading Notes

Contents

Introduction

Oxford Reading Tree stories at Stages 5 to 9 continue to feature the familiar characters from previous stages in stories that reflect the experiences of most children. The magic key, discovered at Stage 4, also takes children into exciting fantasy adventures, widening and enriching their reading experience.

The stories still use natural language, phonically decodable words and high frequency words, all illustrated with funny and engaging pictures. Reading them will enable children to practise different reading skills, and continue to develop their word recognition and language comprehension.

Using the books

This booklet provides suggestions for using the books for guided, group and independent activities. The reading activities include ideas for developing children's *word recognition* **W** and *language comprehension* **C** skills. Within word recognition, there are ideas for helping children practise their phonic skills and knowledge, as well as helping them to tackle words that are not easy to decode phonically. The language comprehension ideas include suggestions for teaching the skills of prediction, questioning, clarifying, summarising and imagining in order to help children understand the text and the whole stories. Suggestions are also provided for speaking, listening, drama and writing activities.

Reading fluency

To support children in developing fluency in their reading, give them plenty of opportunities to revisit the stories. This includes
- rereading independently
- rereading with a partner
- rereading at home

Curriculum coverage chart

	Speaking, listening, drama	Reading	Writing
In the Garden			
PNS Literacy Framework (Y2)	1.1, 2.3, 4.1	**W** 5.2, 5.4, 5.5 **C** 7.2	9.2, 9.4, 10.2, 11.3
National Curriculum	Working towards Level 1		
Scotland (5–14)	Level A	Level A	Level A
N. Ireland (P3/Y3)	1, 2, 3, 5, 6, 7, 8, 9, 10	1, 3, 5, 8, 11, 12, 13, 14, 16, 17	1, 2, 10, 11, 12, 13
Wales (Key Stage 1)	Range: 1, 2, 3 Skills: 1, 2, 3, 4, 5, 6	Range: 1, 2, 4, 5, 6 Skills: 1, 2, 3	Range: 1, 2, 3, 4, 5, Skills: 1, 4, 5, 8
Kipper and the Giant			
PNS Literacy Framework (Y2)	3.3, 4.1	**W** 5.2 **C** 7.2, 7.5, 8.3	9.2, 10.2, 11.1
National Curriculum	Working towards Level 2		
Scotland (5–14)	Level A	Level A	Level A
N. Ireland (P3/Y3)	1, 6, 8, 10, 12	1, 3, 8, 11, 12, 14, 15, 16, 17	1, 2, 7, 10, 11, 12, 13
Wales (Key Stage 1)	Range: 1, 2, 3, 5 Skills: 1, 2, 3	Range: 1, 2, 4, 5, 6 Skills: 1, 2	Range: 1, 2, 3, 4, 7 Skills: 1, 2, 4, 7, 8

Key

C = Language comprehension   Y = Year

W = Word recognition   P = Primary

In the designations such as 5.2, the first number represents the strand and the second number the bullet point

Curriculum coverage chart

	Speaking, listening, drama	Reading	Writing
The Outing			
PNS Literacy Framework (Y2)	1.1, 2.3, 3.2	**W** 5.2, 5.5 **C** 7.4, 8.2	9.1, 9.5
National Curriculum	Working towards Level 2		
Scotland (5–14)	Level A	Level A	Level A
N. Ireland (P3/Y3)	1, 5, 6, 8	1, 3, 5, 8, 11, 12, 14, 15, 16, 17	1, 2, 3, 8, 10, 11, 12
Wales (Key Stage 1)	Range: 1, 2, 3 Skills: 1, 2, 3, 4, 5	Range: 1, 2, 4, 5, 6 Skills: 1, 2	Range: 1, 2, 3, 4, 5 Skills: 1, 3, 4, 7, 8
Land of the Dinosaurs			
PNS Literacy Framework (Y2)	1.1, 2.1, 4.1, 4.2	**W** 6.1, **C** 7.1, 8.2	9.2, 9.4, 10.2, 11.1
National Curriculum	Working towards Level 2		
Scotland (5–14)	Level A	Level A	Level A
N. Ireland (P3/Y3)	1, 2, 6, 10, 11, 12	1, 3, 5, 8, 11, 12, 14, 15, 16, 17	1, 2, 10, 11, 12, 13
Wales (Key Stage 1)	Range: 1, 2, 3, 5, 6 Skills: 1, 2, 3, 4, 5	Range: 1, 2, 4, 5, 6 Skills: 1, 2	Range: 1, 2, 3 Skills: 1, 2, 3, 6, 7, 8

Curriculum coverage chart

	Speaking, listening, drama	Reading	Writing
Robin Hood			
PNS Literacy Framework (Y2)	2.1, 4.1	**W** 6.1 **C** 7.2, 8.3	9.2, 10.1, 11.3
National Curriculum	Working towards Level 2		
Scotland (5–14)	Level A	Level A	Level A
N. Ireland (P3/Y3)	1, 2, 6, 8, 10, 11, 12	1, 3, 5, 8, 11, 12, 14, 15, 16, 17	1, 2, 3, 8, 10, 11, 12, 13
Wales (Key Stage 1)	Range: 1, 2, 3, 5, 6 Skills: 1, 2, 3, 4	Range: 1, 2, 4, 5, 6 Skills: 1, 2	Range: 1, 2, 3, 4, 5 Skills: 1, 2, 3, 7, 8
The Treasure Chest			
PNS Literacy Framework (Y2)	2.3, 4.2	**W** 5.2 **C** 7.1, 7.2	9.5, 10.1
National Curriculum	Working towards Level 2		
Scotland (5–14)	Level A	Level A	Level A
N. Ireland (P3/Y3)	1, 2, 7, 8, 9	1, 3, 5, 8, 11, 12, 14, 15, 16, 17	1, 2, 3, 8, 10, 11, 13
Wales (Key Stage 1)	Range: 1, 2, 3, 5, 6 Skills: 1, 2, 3, 4, 5, 6	Range: 1, 2, 4, 5, 6 Skills: 1, 2, 3	Range: 1, 2, 3, 5, 7 Skills: 1, 2, 7, 8

In the Garden

> **C** = Language comprehension   *W, AF* = QCA writing assessment focus
>
> **W** = Word recognition   *R, AF* = QCA reading assessment focus

Group or guided reading

Introducing the book

C *(Questioning)* Read the title together. Look at the illustration on the front cover. Ask the children: *Do you think the grass and flowers are big, or are the children small?* Start to look through the book. Ask: *Which page can you find out the answer?* (page 5).

- Continue to look through the book and talk about what is happening.

Strategy check

Remind children to move their bookmark so that they can see the words before they get to them.

Independent reading

- Ask children to read the story aloud. Praise and encourage them while they read, and prompt as necessary.

C *(Summarising)* Ask children to retell the story in as few sentences as possible.

Assessment Check that children:

- *(R, AF1)* read high frequency words with confidence
- *(R, AF1)* use a range of strategies to work out new words.

Returning to the text

C *(Questioning, Clarifying)* Ask children: *Why did Kipper say 'Oh no!' when Biff suggested they go down to the 'desert'?*

C *(Imagining)* Ask children to describe what might have happened if Floppy had not frightened the cat away.

C *(Clarifying)* Ask children to explain what the jungle, the hill and the desert actually were.

(W) If children have difficulty reading compound words, e.g. 'sandpit, 'flowerpot', encourage them to find the smaller words within them first.

Group and independent reading activities

Objective Spell with increasing accuracy and confidence, drawing on word recognition and knowledge of spelling patterns (5.2).

(W) Write 'name', 'play' and 'train' on the board.

- Discuss the long vowel phoneme and the different spelling patterns.
- Ask the children to look through the story and find five other words that have the same long 'a' sound, discuss the spelling patterns and group them accordingly ('playing', 'away'; 'came', 'chased', 'ate'; 'rain').
- Do the same with the long 'e' phoneme. Ask the children to find the words and then group according to the spelling, e.g. 'bee' and 'seat'.

Assessment *(R, AF1)* Can children identify the phoneme? Can they group the different spelling patterns?

Objective Read and spell less common alternative graphemes including trigraphs (5.4).

(W) On page 9, ask children to help you read the word 'climb' by blending the phonemes. Explain how the 'b' is silent.

- On page 15, ask a child to show you how to read 'frightened' and discuss in the same way.
- Ask children to find other words in the text with the same vowel phoneme sound 'i–e', e.g. 'like', 'ride', 'giant'.

Assessment *(R, AF1)* Can the children show you how to read 'mountain' on page 8 and 'strawberries' on page 19?

Objective Read high frequency words automatically (5.5).

(W) On pages 6–7, ask children to find 'were' and then 'here'.

- Ask how the pronunciation of the words differs.
- Ask: *What words can you think of that rhyme with 'were'?* ('fur', 'sir'). Write the suggestions down and note the different spelling patterns.
- Repeat with 'here' ('near', 'dear', 'deer').

Assessment *(R, AF1)* Can children find the words 'were', 'want' and 'with' in a collection of flashcards, or among other words written down?

Objective Give some reasons why things happen (7.2).

C *(Questioning)* Ask questions to help children understand how the story develops, e.g. *Why did the children leave the jungle? Why did they climb inside the bottle? Why did Kipper and Chip feel sick?*

Assessment *(R, AF2)* Can children retrieve information from the story?

Objective Use appropriate language to make sections hang together (10.2).

C *(Clarifying)* Write the following sentences on the board:

They came to a mountain.
Floppy chased the cat away.
The children were in the grass.

● Ask the children to say the order in which the above events happened, using 'First', 'Next' and 'Last'.

● Ask the children to choose three other sentences from the story and write them using 'First', 'Next' and 'Last'.

Assessment *(W, AF3)* Do the children choose sentences that show a sequence of events? Do they remember to use capital letters and full stops?

Objective Engage with books through exploring and enacting interpretations (8.2). Make adventurous word and language choices (9.4).

C *(Imagining)* Ask the children to imagine they are as tiny as the characters in the story and to then write notes/sentences on what it would be like if they were that small in their own garden, local park or their bedroom.

● What hazards would they face?

● Encourage children to use imaginative and descriptive language.

● Brainstorm some words to put on the board (e.g. 'terrified', 'scared stiff', 'spooked').

Assessment *(W, AF2)* Can children describe a scary event?

Speaking, listening and drama activities

Objective Respond to presentations by describing characters and commenting constructively (2.3). Adopt appropriate roles in small groups and consider alternative courses of action (4.1).

● In small groups, ask the children to re-enact the incident in the story involving the cat.

- Ask one child to volunteer to be the cat and the rest of the group the children.
- Encourage the children to explore the behaviour of the cat. (inquisitive) and the behaviour of the children (frightened).
- Invite groups to act out their scene to the rest of the class. Encourage the audience to make constructive comments on how successfully the group convey the feelings of the children and the cat.
- Ask the children to think of alternative ways that the characters could have escaped the cat.

Objective Speak with clarity and use appropriate intonation when reading and reciting texts (1.1).

- Ask children to read pages 8–17 with a partner, each child reading alternate pages.
- Tell them to read the words in the way they think the characters would say them, speaking clearly and with expression.

Writing activities

Objective Sustain form in narrative, including use of time (9.2). Use appropriate language to make sections hang together (10.2).

- Write some time language on the board, e.g. 'First…', 'Meanwhile', 'After', 'Suddenly' 'At last'.
- Ask the children to use the notes they compiled in the earlier activity to write a story about being tiny in their own garden, park or bedroom using the language of time to show the sequence of events.

Assessment *(W, AF2)* Can children sequence the information in the story effectively?

Objective Use commas to separate items in a list (11.3).

- Turn to pages 2–3. Ask the children to look at the picture and tell you all things they can see, e.g. cat, toy car, tin can, sandcastle.
- Write the words on the board.
- Ask the children to complete the following sentence, listing all the items they can see in the picture:
  In the garden I can see a…
- Show them how to separate each item with a comma.

Assessment *(W, AF6)* Do children separate the items in a list with commas?

Kipper and the Giant

> **C** = Language comprehension   *R, AF* = QCA reading assessment focus
>
> **W** = Word recognition   *W, AF* = QCA writing assessment focus

Group or guided reading

Introducing the book

C *(Prediction)* Look at the illustration on the front cover together. Read the title and the blurb on the back cover. Ask the children: *Who do you think will be the giant in the story?*

C *(Clarifying)* Look briefly through the story up to page 9 to confirm the children's ideas.

● Continue to look through the book and talk about what is happening.

Strategy check

Remind the children to sound out and blend the phonemes to work out new words.

Independent reading

● Ask children to read the story. Praise and encourage them while they read, and prompt as necessary.

C *(Clarifying)* On pages 10–11 ask: *Why don't the people like Kipper? Did he do anything wrong?*

C *(Summarising)* Ask children to retell the story in as few sentences as possible.

Assessment Check that children:

● *(R, AF1)* read high frequency words on sight

● *(R, AF3)* understand the reasons why Kipper wasn't liked by the villagers at first.

Returning to the text

C *(Imagining)* Ask: *If Kipper hadn't started crying what might have happened?*

C *(Clarifying)* Turn to page 2, ask: *What is the giant doing to show that he is cross?*

(C) (*Questioning*) Ask children to describe in what way Kipper was useful to the villagers. What advantage did he have over them?

(C) (*Clarifying*) Ask the children to explain why we know that the giant has been on holiday (see page 6).

(C) (*Clarifying*) Turn to page 20 and read the first line. Ask: *Why does it say 'but' and not 'and' here?*

(W) Ask the children to look back through the book and find some long words. Can they find a word with four syllables? ('television', page 1).

(W) Ask the children to tell you how they worked out the new words 'signpost' and 'village' (page 7), 'perhaps' (page 13), 'bandage' (page 20). Praise them for splitting the words up into syllables then sounding out and blending the phonemes. Ask: *What two words make up the word 'signpost'?*

Group and independent reading activities

Objective Listen to each other's views (3.3). Give some reasons why things happen or characters change (7.2).

(C) (*Questioning, Clarifying*)

- Write the following questions on the board:
  Why did Kipper run to get Biff?
  Why did Kipper go to the village?
  Why did Kipper begin to cry?
  Why did the villagers say 'Good old Kipper'?
  Why was the giant very angry?
- Ask the children, in pairs, to look through the book to find the answers to the questions and discuss them together.
- Ask each child to write a new question, swap it with a partner's question and then write the answer to that question, referring to the book if necessary.

Assessment (*R, AF2*) Are the children able to identify the reasons for the things Kipper does in the story?

Objective Use appropriate language to make sections hang together (10.2). Write simple and compound sentences and use subordination in relation to time (11.1).

W Discuss with the children the sorts of words that can be used to join sentences and show a sequence of events, e.g. 'next', 'then', 'before' and 'after'.

● Together draw up a list for the children to use in their own writing.
● Write on the board 'Kipper went to the village'.

C *(Clarifying)* Ask the children to write what happens next in the story, using words from the prepared list to link their sentences.

Assessment (W, AF3) Can children sequence information effectively?

Objective Spell with increasing accuracy and confidence, drawing on word recognition and knowledge of word structure, and spelling patterns (5.2).

W Write the word 'like' on the board.

● Discuss the long vowel phoneme 'ie'.

● Ask the children to collect words from the story with the same long vowel phoneme and group them according to spelling pattern, e.g. 'i–e': 'time', 'inside', 'outside'; 'igh': 'frightened'; 'y': 'cry', 'try'; 'i': 'find', 'tiny'.

● Draw up a table on a large piece of paper. Write in the words the children have found under the appropriate spelling pattern.

● Ask the children to add to the poster other words with the same spelling patterns and vowel sound.

● Display the poster and ask the children to add new words when they find them.

● Ask children to find words that have the short vowel phoneme 'i', e.g. 'lived', 'in', 'picked'.

Assessment (R, AF1) Can the children differentiate between long and short vowel sounds and spellings?

Objective Explore how particular words are used, including words with similar meanings (7.5).

C *(Clarifying)* Ask the children to find words in the book that describe the Giant's character (e.g. pages 1 and 18: 'angry'; pages 2 and 3: 'cross').

● Ask: *Can you think of any other words the author could have used?*
● Compile a list.

- *What about words to describe the giant at the end of the story?*

Assessment *(W, AF7)* Can the children use different words with the same meaning to describe someone?

Objective Explain their reactions to texts, commenting on important aspects (8.3).

- **C** *(Clarifying)* Ask the children to turn to pages 12–13.
- Ask: *Are you surprised that Kipper started crying? What would you have done in the same situation?*
- Discuss how for the story to continue it is important that the villagers change their mind about Kipper.

Assessment *(R, AF3)* Can children describe events in stories and make comments about what they have read.

Speaking, listening and drama activities

Objective Adopt appropriate roles in small groups and consider alternative courses of action (4.1).

- Choose some children to take turns to be Kipper and sit in the 'hot seat'.
- Encourage the other children to ask 'Kipper' questions to describe what it is like to be 'a giant' and why he does the things he does.

Writing activities

Objective Sustain form in narrative, including use of time (9.2).

- Ask the children to imagine they are giants and they have come to visit the school for the day.
- Ask them to describe what they see, how it is different from normal and what difficulties they encounter, e.g. low doorways, tiny chairs.
- Allow the children to role play being a giant if it helps them to describe the actions. Ask the children to write a description of their visit, e.g. what they do when they arrive, where they eat lunch, what they do in the afternoon and when they leave.

Assessment *(W, AF3)* Can children sequence the information in the story effectively?

The Outing

> **C** = Language comprehension   **R, AF** = QCA reading assessment focus
>
> **W** = Word recognition   **W, AF** = QCA writing assessment focus

Group or guided reading

Introducing the book

C *(Prediction)* Look at the front cover together and discuss what is happening. Ask the children to read the back cover blurb and say what they think will happen in the story.

C *(Clarifying)* Ask the children to look briefly through the story to find out where the characters go.

Strategy check

Remind the children how to tackle unfamiliar words that are not completely decodable.

Independent reading

● Ask children to read the story. Praise and encourage them while they read, and prompt as necessary.

W If children struggle with the word 'apatosaurus' on page 15, suggest they break it down into syllables.

C *(Summarising)* Ask children to retell the story in as few sentences as possible.

Assessment   Check that children:

● *(R, AF1)* use a range of strategies to work out new words

● *(R, AF3)* understand why the characters went to the museum

● *(R, AF3)* read with expression appropriate to the grammar and punctuation.

Returning to the text

C *(Questioning)* Ask: *What did Wilf lose? What did Nadim bring back?*

C *(Clarifying)* On page 24, ask: *How does Chip know they are going to the land of the dinosaurs?*

(C) (Prediction) Ask: *What do you think might happen in the land of the dinosaurs?*

(W) Ask children to find words in the book with the phoneme 'f' spelt 'ph' ('elephants' page 9, 'photograph' page 15). Can the children think of any other words? Provide a dictionary for more able children to look up 'ph' words.

(W) Turn to page 2. Ask the children to look at what Mrs May says. Discuss why there is an apostrophe in 'we're' and 'don't'. Talk about how in informal written speech some words are joined together, in the way that we say them.

(C) (Questioning) Ask the children to count the number of times Mrs May says 'don't'. Ask: *Why does Mrs May keep saying this? Is she worried? What is she worried about? Do you think the children are taking much notice of Mrs May?*

(W) Find 'stopped' on page 4. Ask: *What is the root word?* (stop). *What has been added to make it a word to show it happened in the past?* ('p' and 'ed'). Ask the children to see if they can find other words that change when in the past tense ('told', 'ran'). Ask them to make a list of words that stay the same but just have 'ed' added.

Group and independent reading activities

Objective Speak with clarity (1.1). Respond to presentations by commenting constructively (2.3). Engage with books through exploring and enacting interpretations (8.2).

(C) (Summarising) Ask the children to work with a partner and to take turns to retell the story to each other.

● The children then look through the story and compare with their versions.

● Ask some children to read out their versions of the story to the group.

● Discuss the differences between the retellings.

Assessment (R, AF3) Are the children able to retell the story in sequence?

Objective Speak with clarity and use appropriate intonation when reading and reciting texts (1.1). Work effectively in groups by ensuring that each group member takes a turn challenging, supporting and moving on (3.2).

(W) Ask the children to work with a partner and to take turns to read only the spoken words in the story.

- Encourage them to use expression appropriate to the punctuation used in the text.
- As a group, discuss what helps the children to read with expression, e.g. exclamation marks.

Assessment *(R, AF6)* Do children pause at commas and change their tone according to the punctuation?

Objective Spell with increasing accuracy and confidence (5.2). Read high and medium frequency words independently and automatically (5.5). Use syntax and context to build their store of vocabulary when reading for meaning (7.4).

(W) Write the following sentences on the board:

We're going…the zoo.
Don't go…near the water.
We all wear…shoes.

- Discuss the three words 'to', 'too' and 'two'.
- Ask the children to read the sentences on the board, then write them, filling in each gap with the correct word.
- Ask them to skim through the book and find examples of 'to' and 'too' and read the sentences they appear in.
- Ask them to write their own sentences using 'to', too' and 'two' correctly.

Assessment *(R, AF3)* Can the children write three new sentences using the different words correctly?

Speaking, listening and drama activities

Objective Work effectively in groups by ensuring that each group member takes a turn (3.2).

- Sit with the children in a circle and discuss what Wilf did near the water on page 6 of the story.
- Ask the children to think about the dangers of water and, in turn, ask each child to contribute to a list of what not to do near water.
- Ask children for ideas on how playing near water could be made safe and list them.

Writing activities

Objective Draw on knowledge and experience of texts in deciding and planning what and how to write (9.1).

- Ask the children to tell you what happened in the story, and write a simplified version on the board in notes.
- Discuss which parts of the story would stay the same if it were being written about different children who went on a different outing, e.g. to a farm park or the seaside.
- Using the parts identified by the children, write them as a framework to help the children structure their own writing about a different outing.

Assessment *(W, AF2)* Can children produce texts which are appropriate to task?

Objective Select from different presentational features to suit particular writing purposes on paper and on screen (9.5).

- Using a computer program, e.g. Word, or paper, ask the children to write a letter from one of the characters in the story to Mrs May, thanking her for his or her day out.
- Talk about the kind of things that might be included in the letter, e.g. what part of the day the character liked best, anything funny that happened, anything new they learned.
- Design a letter template in Word or discuss how to lay out a simple letter with the date, etc.

Assessment *(W, AF2)* Can children produce texts which are appropriate to task?

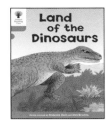

Land of the Dinosaurs

C = Language comprehension   *R, AF* = QCA reading assessment focus

W = Word recognition   *W, AF* = QCA writing assessment focus

Group or guided reading

Introducing the book

C *(Prediction)* Look at the front cover together and discuss what is happening. Ask the children to read the back cover blurb and say what they think will happen in the story.

Strategy check

Remind the children to reread the whole sentence when they get stuck on a word.

Independent reading

● Ask children to read the story. Praise and encourage them while they read, and prompt as necessary. Encourage them to read with expression.

W If children get stuck on the tricky words 'enormous' on page 14 and 'fierce' on page 19, help them to sound out and blend the phonemes.

C *(Questioning, Clarifying)* Ask questions to help children's understanding of the story, e.g.: *Why is Wilf wearing a plastic bag on one foot? (page 2); Why do you think the dinosaur looks startled on page 16?*

Assessment Check that children:

● *(R, AF1)* read high frequency words with fluency and confidence

● *(R, AF4)* take account of the grammar and punctuation while reading aloud

● *(R, AF4)* are able to use the sense and structure of the sentence to decipher new words.

Returning to the text

C *(Summarising)* Ask the children to describe the creature the children met first. *What did they meet next? Which one was after that? Which was*

the last dinosaur they met? Why didn't they see any more? Retell the sequence together using 'first', 'next', 'then' and 'after that'.

(W) On page 7, find 'egg' and 'eggs'. Ask: *What is the difference in the spelling? What is the difference in the meaning?* Ask children to find other examples of words in the book where an 's' has been added to make it plural (dinosaurs, photographs).

(W) Introduce the possessive apostrophe to more able children. Ask the children to find 'dinosaur's eggs' on page 6. Ask: *What does this mean? How is it different to adding an 's' to a word without the apostrophe?*

(C) *(Imagining)* Ask the children to imagine what would have happened if Biff had been able to develop some photographs to take to school. Would anyone have believed Biff?

(C) *(Clarifying, Imagining)* Talk about why Wilf's shoes keep coming off. Ask: *Is Wilf's mum going to be pleased with him?*

Group and independent reading activities

Objective Draw together ideas and information from across a whole text (7.1). Sustain form in narrative, including use of time (9.2).

(C) *(Summarising)* **You will need** word cards for 'firstly', 'immediately', 'meanwhile', 'after that', 'suddenly', 'next' and 'then'.

● On strips of card write out the following sentences:
A dinosaur flew down.
Nadim found some eggs.
Chip found a footprint.
Wilf ran on and climbed a hill.
Biff took a photograph.
A little dinosaur came out of the egg.
Biff picked up a stick.

● Ask the children to put the sentence strips in the right order, and to start each one with one of the word cards.

● Alternatively, type the words and sentences into a word processing software and ask the children to drag and drop the words into the sentences.

Assessment *(R, AF3)* Do the children need to refer to the story to sequence the sentences?

Objective Speak with clarity when reading (1.1). Engage with books through exploring and enacting interpretations (8.2). Write simple and compound sentences (11.1).

- Ask the children to look through the book at the illustrations and to choose the one they like best.

- **C** *(Clarifying)* Ask them to write two new sentences to go with the picture.

- Encourage them to read their sentences aloud and to check they make sense.

Assessment *(W, AF6)* Do children begin their sentences with a capital letter and end with a full stop?

Objective Spell with increasing accuracy and confidence, including use of double letters (6.1).

- **W** Ask the children to find as many words as they can that have a double 'l', e.g. 'silly', 'hill', 'called', 'yelled', 'well'.

- Repeat with words with double 'g': 'egg', 'bigger'. Ask: *Why is another 'g' added to 'big' to make 'bigger'? How would it read if it was 'biger'? What other words have a double 'g'?* ('digger', 'digging', 'begging', 'foggy').

Assessment *(W, AF8)* Do children spell words with double letters accurately?

Speaking, listening and drama activities

Objective Listen to others in class, ask relevant questions (2.1). Adopt appropriate roles in small or large groups (4.1).

- **C** *(Questioning)* Talk about what Biff does when the dinosaur egg hatches.

- Ask the children to create a series of freeze frames to show the incident (pages 8–12).

- Ask the children to take turns to be Biff and sit in the 'hot seat'.

- Ask the other children to think of a question to ask 'Biff' about what she did.

- Draw out from the children whether they thought what Biff did in the book was sensible.

- Ask: *What would they have done in the same situation? Was Chip right to have told Biff off?*

Objective Listen to others in class, ask relevant questions (2.1). Present part of stories for members of their own class (4.2).

- In small groups, ask children to choose one part of the story which they found funny or scary, or both, e.g. the children being chased by the dinosaur and Wilf's shoe coming off.
- Ask them to act out their chosen scene and perform it to the class. Encourage the children to adopt the correct expressions.
- Invite the audience at the end to ask the group questions about the choice of scene, e.g. 'Why did you choose that scene?'

Writing activities

Objective Sustain form in narrative, including use of time (9.2). Use appropriate language to make sections hang together (10.2). Write simple and compound sentences (11.1).

- **You will need** time connective words written on cards: 'first', 'then', 'next', 'after that', 'in the end', etc.
- Ask the children, in pairs, to discuss the story and to pick six key events to write a sentence about, using the book if necessary.
- Tell the children to pick a word card to begin their sentences, and to make sure that the sentences show the correct sequence.

Assessment *(W, AF3)* Can children sequence information effectively?

Objective Make adventurous word and language choices appropriate to the style and purpose of the text (9.4).

- With the children, brainstorm new words to describe one dramatic incident in the book, e.g. the flying dinosaur attacking the baby dinosaur.
- Encourage the children to write two or three sentences describing the event using some of the new words, e.g. 'The fierce dinosaur with its sharp teeth, attacked the lonely baby dinosaur...'

Assessment *(W, AF7)* Do children attempt new and imaginative words to describe an event?

Robin Hood

> **C** = Language comprehension   *R, AF* = QCA reading assessment focus
>
> **W** = Word recognition   *W, AF* = QCA writing assessment focus

Group or guided reading

Introducing the book

C *(Prediction)* Look at the front cover together. Ask the children what they think the story is about.

● Ask them to read the blurb on the back cover. Discuss what the children know about Robin Hood and what they think will happen in the story.

Strategy check

Remind the children to blend phonemes to read new, longer words.

Independent reading

● Ask children to read the story. Praise and encourage them while they read, and prompt as necessary. Praise them for rereading if a sentence does not make sense first time round.

W Discuss why 'is' is written in italics on page 9 and refer back to the text about Robin Hood on page 2.

Assessment Check that children:

● *(R, AF1)* read high frequency words with fluency and confidence
● *(R, AF1)* use a range of strategies to work out new words.

Returning to the text

C *(Questioning, Clarifying)* Turn to page 1 and ask: *What is a pantomime? Where do you go to see a pantomime? Have you ever been to one?*

W Ask the children to show you how they read the word 'Sheriff' on page 3. Did they sound out the phonemes and then blend (sh–e–r–i–ff)?

C *(Clarifying)* Ask: *What instruments were the girls playing on pages 4–5?*

W Ask the children to show you the words for the instruments on page 4 and tell you how many syllables are in each word.

- Ask: *Where did you notice capital letters in the story?* Look at the pictures on pages 1and 5. Discuss the reasons for them. Ask: *Why is there a capital letter on Biff? What are initials? What are your initials?*

- Ask the children to find a question mark on page 10. Ask: *Who is speaking? Why doesn't the last sentence have a question mark?*

- **C** *(Questioning)* On page 23, ask: *Why did Kipper say 'Just in time' when the key started to glow?*

Group and independent reading activities

Objective Give some reasons why things happen (7.2). Sustain form in narrative, including use of time (9.2).

- **C** *(Summarising)* Invite children to summarise the story in four sentences. Compare summaries and agree the key points of the story.

- Write 'What happened when...' on the board.

- Ask the children: *When is the first time Biff sings a song about Robin Hood? Why do you think she sang it?* If necessary, talk about how the characters had been to see the Robin Hood pantomime the night before. Ask: *How do we know it is the next day when she sang the song?* Prompt the children to find 'The next day' on page 4.

- Ask the children to work in pairs and to think of questions beginning 'What happened when...'. Children take it in turns to ask each other questions referring to the book when necessary.

Assessment *(R, AF3)* Do the children understand that the characters' actions affect the plot? Do they realise that an event occurs because of what has happened before?

Objective Spell with increasing accuracy and confidence, drawing on word recognition and spelling patterns (6.1).

- **W** Discuss the 'oo' sound in Robin Hood with the children. Ask them to find other words in the story with the same spelling, e.g. 'good', 'wood', 'took', 'looked', 'goodbye', 'woooooooh' and 'too'.

- Discuss the differences in the 'oo' sound between some of the words, e.g. short phoneme sound in 'good' and the long phoneme sound in 'too'.

- Write the words that the children found in two lists.
- Ask the children to use word banks or dictionaries to find and group other words with the same spelling but different sounds.
- What words can the children think of that have the long vowel phoneme 'oo' but are spelt differently, e.g. 'glue', 'do', 'you'.
- Encourage them to compile their own lists.

Assessment *(R, AF1)* Do children add new words that they find to the right list?

Objective Explain their reactions to texts, commenting on important aspects (8.3).

C *(Questioning)* Ask the children to describe what they think of Robin Hood in the story.

- Prompt them to use words like 'good', 'kind'.
- Ask: *Does the story make him out to be a hero? Who saved him? What can we learn about him when he says, 'Now let's sing that song about me again.'?* (page 22).
- Discuss whether he is rather full of his own importance or if he is just enjoying the way the children are singing the song.
- Ask the children to draw a picture of Robin Hood and write a brief character profile of him based on information from the story.

Assessment *(R, AF3)* Can children deduce information from the story and make their own opinion?

Speaking, listening and drama activities

Objective Listen to others in class, ask relevant questions (2.1). Adopt appropriate roles in small or large groups (4.1).

- Invite some children in turn to take the role of Kipper and sit in the 'hot seat'.
- Ask 'Kipper' to tell the group what happened when he met Robin Hood.
- Encourage the other children to ask 'Kipper' questions about his experiences.

Writing activities

Objective Sustain form in narrative, including use of time (9.2). Use planning to establish clear sections for writing (10.1).

- Write the following time connectives on the board: 'first', 'next', 'then', 'after that', and 'suddenly'.

- Ask the children to turn to the part in the story where Kipper rescues everyone (pages 18–21).

- Ask the children to use the illustrations as a stimulus for their writing. Encourage them to plan their sentences by writing notes under the time connective headings, e.g. 'First', 'Next':

'First'
First Kipper walked up to the soldier.
He asked the soldier what the thing was.
The soldier explained.

'Next'
Next the soldier showed Kipper how it worked.

- Remind the children that they can add different connectives or change them around if they wish.

Assessment *(W, AF3)* Can children sequence information effectively?

Objective Use question marks (11.3).

- In pairs, ask the children to think of questions they might want to ask Robin Hood if they were one of the children in the story.

- If necessary make a list of question words on the board for the children to refer to, e.g. 'what', 'where', 'when'.

- You or a volunteer child take the role of Robin Hood and the children ask their questions for you to answer.

Assessment *(W, AF6)* Do the children use question marks correctly?

The Treasure Chest

C = Language comprehension   *R, AF* = QCA reading assessment focus

W = Word recognition   *W, AF* = QCA writing assessment focus

Group or guided reading

Introducing the book

C *(Prediction)* Look at the front cover together. Ask the children what they think the story is about. Ask them to read the title and the blurb on the back cover. Ask the children: *What do you think will happen in the story? Do you think the children will meet an octopus?*

Strategy check

Remind the children to take note of punctuation and to read with expression.

Independent reading

- Ask children to read the story. Praise and encourage them while they read, and prompt as necessary.

C *(Clarifying)* On page 17, ask the children what is happening in the illustration. Ask them to read the word 'different' and say how this adventure is different.

C *(Clarifying)* On page 19, ask why the text says 'thought' instead of 'said'.

Assessment Check that children:

- *(R, AF1)* read high frequency words with fluency
- *(R, AF1)* use a variety of cues to decipher new words
- *(R, AF3)* read with expression appropriate to the grammar and punctuation.

Returning to the text

C *(Questioning)* On page 32, ask: *Why were the children surprised to see the treasure chest in the tank? Do you think it was magic? Do you think Mum and Dad will think it was magic?*

C *(Summarising)* Ask: *What was the most exciting part of the story? On which page is it? What was exciting about it?*

W Explain that there are some words that sound the same but are spelt differently and have different meanings. Suggest they look at page 1 and find the word 'some'. Ask: *Who knows another word that sounds like 'some'?* (sum). Write the word down. *What does it mean?*

W In the same way, find the word 'there' on page 15 and ask for another word that sounds like 'there' (their). Do the same for 'new' on page 17 (knew). Discuss the meanings of all the words.

Group and independent reading activities

Objective Give some reasons why things happen (7.2).

C *(Questioning, Summarising)* Ask the children to think about three key things that happen in the story, and list them on the board, e.g. the children pass a swimming test; the children and Dad go shopping for more things for their fish tank; the children have an underwater adventure.

● Ask each child to choose one event and write a sentence explaining the reason why it happened using the word 'because'.

● Ask children to think up any questions they might like to ask the characters in the story. Discuss possible answers.

Assessment *(R, AF3)* Do the children understand that using 'because' shows cause and effect?

Objective Draw together ideas and information from across a whole text (7.1).

C *(Clarifying)* **You will need** photocopies of the following list of sentences (with at least three line spaces between each sentence):

The magic began to work.
They saw an octopus sitting on a chest.
They swam up to the ship.
The children could swim underwater.
They saw a ship under the water.
The octopus swam away.
It was full of gold.
The children opened the chest.

- Give out the sheets to the children and ask them to cut them up and reorder them so they are in the correct sequence.
- Suggest that they stick the sentences down on another piece of paper.
- Ask the children to write a sentence that follows on from the last sentence in the sequence.

Assessment *(W, AF3)* Can children order the sentences without referring to the story?

Objective Spell with increasing accuracy and confidence, drawing on word recognition and knowledge of word structure, and spelling patterns (5.2).

W Ask the children to look at the illustration on pages 18–19 and to say what colours they can see. Encourage them to write down the list of colours.

- Compile a list on the board asking for spelling suggestions.
- Ask: *Which words are trickier to spell, what will help us?* Encourage children to suggest different strategies.

Assessment *(R, AF1)* Are children able to spell the common colour names?

Speaking, listening and drama activities

Objective Respond to presentations, commenting constructively (2.3). Present part of stories for members of their own class (4.2).

- Discuss how Chip and Wilma had to use sign language to warn Biff and Nadim about the shark.
- Ask the children to prepare and mime a short scenario in small groups, e.g. there has been an accident and they must call an ambulance; a person is struggling in a pool and the life guard rescues them. Remind them that they cannot speak.
- The children mime their prepared plays to an audience.
- Invite the audience to make constructive criticism on how well the children mimed their scene.

Writing activities

Objective Select from different presentational features to suit particular writing purposes on paper (9.5).

- Discuss the swimming test that the children took on pages 4–6 of the story.
- Ask the children to write some instructions explaining what the children had to do to pass the test.
- Note down some of their suggestions on the board using a numbered list, e.g.

The Swimming Test
1. Jump into the pool.
2. Swim ten lengths.

- What other swimming activities could they add to the list? Ask the children to add these in the same instruction format.

Assessment *(W, AF2)* Have the children produced a list of instructions?

Objective Use planning to establish clear sections for writing (10.1).

- Talk about the settings for the story: the swimming pool; the home; underwater in the tank.
- Explain that the children are going to make a plan that would help them to write a brief summary of the story.
- Show how to organise the information using circles and arrows and discuss in which setting the main events of the story occurred, e.g.

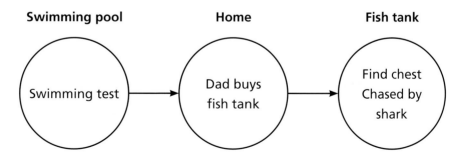

Swimming pool	Home	Fish tank
Swimming test	Dad buys fish tank	Find chest Chased by shark

Assessment *(W, AF3)* Are children able to use their plans to answer questions about the sequence of events in the story?

INSPIRATIONAL SUPPORT FOR TEACHERS
For free professional development videos from leading experts, plus other resources and free eBooks, please go to
www.oxfordprimary.co.uk

HELPING YOU ENGAGE PARENTS
We have researched the most common concerns and worries parents have about their children's literacy and provide answers and support in
www.oxfordowl.co.uk
This site contains advice on how to share a book, how to pronounce pure sounds, how to encourage boys' reading, and much more. We hope you will find the site useful and recommend it to your parents.

OXFORD
UNIVERSITY PRESS

Great Clarendon Street, Oxford OX2 6DP

Oxford University Press is a department of the University of Oxford. It furthers the University's objective of excellence in research, scholarship, and education by publishing worldwide in

Oxford New York
Auckland Cape Town Dar es Salaam Hong Kong Karachi
Kuala Lumpur Madrid Melbourne Mexico City Nairobi
New Delhi Shanghai Taipei Toronto

With offices in

Argentina Austria Brazil Chile Czech Republic France
Greece Guatemala Hungary Italy Japan Poland
Portugal Singapore South Korea Switzerland
Thailand Turkey Ukraine Vietnam

Oxford is a registered trade mark of Oxford University Press in the UK and in certain other countries

Text © Oxford University Press 2008

Written by Lucy Tritton, based on the orginal characters created by Roderick Hunt and Alex Brychta.

The moral rights of the author have been asserted

Database right Oxford University Press (maker)

First published 2008
This edition published 2011

British Library Cataloguing in Publication Data

Data available

Cover illustrations Alex Brychta

ISBN: 978-0-19-848285-7

10 9 8 7 6 5

Page make-up by Thomson Digital

Printed in China by Imago

Paper used in the production of this book is a natural, recyclable product made from wood grown in sustainable forests. The manufacturing process conforms to the environmental regulations of the country of origin.